Original title:
Discovering Purpose... Maybe Tomorrow

Copyright © 2025 Creative Arts Management OÜ
All rights reserved.

Author: Juliette Kensington
ISBN HARDBACK: 978-1-80566-018-7
ISBN PAPERBACK: 978-1-80566-313-3

The Light at the End

I stumbled in a foggy haze,
Chasing dreams in silly ways.
A sign that says, 'You're almost there!'
Oh wait, that's just a grocery fare!

With a map that's upside down,
I search the parks and greet the clown.
He shouts, "Life's a grand old joke!"
I nod and trip on some old smoke.

Each step feels like a dance gone wrong,
I hum a tune that's not quite strong.
But laughter echoes in my wake,
I might just make a giant cake!

So here I roam in silly plight,
In hopes of finding what feels right.
Maybe the answer's in the blue,
Or in the sandwich I won't chew!

Reaching for Tomorrow

I set my sights on dreams so wide,
Like a kid who found a slide.
But my legs are short, I barely reach,
The top, it feels like climbing a peach!

With a telescope aimed at the stars,
I'm convinced I'll find some candy bars.
But it's just a satellite up there,
Whistling tunes that fill the air.

"Tomorrow's here!" I shout with glee,
As I bump my head on a tall pine tree.
My schedule's full of 'maybe' dreams,
But life's as sweet as ice cream themes!

So I sprinkle joy like fairy dust,
And trust in time, it's a must.
I'll laugh and play, make small mistakes,
For in the end, it's just the breaks!

The Nature of Becoming

A caterpillar sighs on a leaf,
Wondering how it got this brief.
"Should I nap or try to soar?"
"What's this fuzz? Is there more?"

With every munch on greens so bright,
It ponders life's grand, goofy flight.
Wings seem nice, but what's the cost?
"If I'm a butterfly, am I lost?"

Dreams in Bloom

In a garden full of wild imagination,
We plant our dreams with slight hesitation.
Sunflowers dance, tulips sway,
"Will I be a bloom or a salad today?"

Petunias giggle as they take a chance,
"Will we color the world, or just make a mess?"
The daisies chime in with hopes so bright,
"Let's aim for the sky, or a pizza tonight!"

Searching for Stardust

One night while gazing up so high,
A star fell and gave a sigh.
"Find my sparkle, follow my trail!"
"But watch out, the moon has a scale!"

With a wink and a cosmic dance,
We gather stardust, take a chance.
"Will I twinkle like soda pop?"
"Or just fizzle and then drop?"

In the Embrace of Dusk

As the sun yawns, and night takes flight,
We stumble into the soft twilight.
"Are the shadows here to stay?
Or will they trip me on the way?"

Crickets chime with a cheeky tune,
"Should we dance under the pale moon?"
With fireflies leading the merry quest,
"Tonight, we'll glow and be our best!"

A Labyrinth of Dreams

In a maze of my own head,
I stumbled on a talking bread.
He said, "Go right for wealth galore,
But left leads to a pizza store!"

With plans just scribbled on the floor,
I chased a cat, ran out the door.
Believe me, I lost my way,
But hey, it's just another day!

Charting New Skies

Set a sail with jelly beans,
I'll navigate through candy dreams.
With marshmallow clouds up high,
I'll trade my boat for a pie!

Unicorns are my compass true,
They prance and dance, not one, but two.
Oh, the maps are drawn in crayon,
But who needs 'em? Just go on!

Moments of Clarity

I woke up one sunny morn,
With socks that are perfectly worn.
Thoughts rushed in like a tidal wave,
Was I wise or just a knave?

My coffee spilled and made a mess,
But it sparked ideas, I confess.
I'll write a book, or maybe two,
A bestseller about my shoe!

Beneath the Surface

In my backyard, I dug too deep,
Searched for treasures, had to leap.
But all I found was my old shoe,
Guess I'll just start anew!

The ground whispered secrets sweet,
Told me that I'm quite the treat.
With garden gnomes as my best friends,
We're plotting out some silly bends!

Moments Between Time

In a world where seconds zip,
I misplace my dreams, I trip.
Chasing shadows in my mind,
Life's a joke, oh, what a grind.

Coffee spills, the clock's a tease,
Sweaters worn on summer's breeze.
If I laugh, will time rewind?
Or am I just a silly blind?

Smiles dance in the fleeting light,
My cat thinks he knows what's right.
I scribble plans that go awry,
As leaves fall, I just sigh.

But in this mess, I find some cheer,
Tomorrow holds a slice of beer.
I'll raise a glass, let laughter roam,
And wander back to call it home.

Awakening to Possibility

Awake, I search for what's afoot,
A sockless shoe, a missing boot.
The cat's advice is far from clear,
Should I pursue, or just stay here?

Plans I write—oh what a jam!
A paper plane, a squawking ham.
If I could pitch my aim, my fate,
Maybe I'd fly, or just sedate.

Balloons float by, and I just wave,
What secrets lie in jesting brave?
My phone chirps with a flirty ping,
Yet who knows what tomorrow brings?

So here I sit with dreams in tow,
And try to steer, or just let go.
With laughter loud, I twirl around,
In silly moments, joy is found.

The Heart's Odyssey

In search of love, I lost my keys,
Unlocked my heart but not my cheese.
I wander streets with hopeful grace,
As pigeons stare, I hide my face.

A date with fate, I dress to kill,
But tripped on air, went down the hill.
I laughed so hard it turned to snorts,
The heart's a boat, and I'm in shorts.

If laughter's love, then I am rich,
I'll write a song and whistle a pitch.
Tomorrow's chance might come around,
But today's laughter is where I'm found.

So here I roam in clumsy style,
With every stutter, I'll make you smile.
For in this heart, adventure brews,
Where every misstep sings the blues.

A Quiet Revelation

In whispers soft, the thoughts parade,
My mind's a curious masquerade.
With socks that clash and mismatched shoes,
My life's a puzzle—pick and choose.

The cat ponders deep philosophy,
Should I bake cookies, or just flee?
Ideas bounce like balls in air,
While my lunch grows cold—beyond compare.

If quiet's gold, I'm broke as can be,
Yet laughter's riches flow so free.
I meditate on cheese and bread,
And seek the peace where roads have led.

Tomorrow hints at jests and grace,
In playful joy, I find my place.
With every giggle, I inch ahead,
In calm revelations, I'm gently led.

Uncharted Dreams

In the land of socks and mismatched shoes,
I ponder what to do with my Tuesday blues.
Should I bake a cake or dance with a broom?
Life's a mystery, in my cluttered room.

The cat sits judging, with a snooty stare,
While I wear a hat that's quite beyond compare.
I flip through fantasies and snack too much,
Maybe I'll call a llama for a chat, oh such!

The Whispering Path

One day I'll wander down the street so wide,
Where squirrels debate on how to best hide.
With ice cream cones and a skateboard's glide,
I'll chase wild thoughts that frolic and bide.

My shoes might squeak like a cheesy old tune,
I'll jest with the sun and dance with the moon.
Each step I'll take, the giggles arise,
In this silly realm, where laughter's the prize.

Beneath the Starlit Veil

Under the stars, I'll trade my old fears,
With a wink and a grin, I'll chuckle through tears.
Aliens might watch as I twirl 'round a tree,
If they join the dance, that'd be quite the spree!

I'll twinkle my toes on a cloud made of dreams,
And plot silly schemes with my rogue moonbeams.
I might even fly on a butterfly's wing,
In this whimsical night, where absurdities sing.

Echoes of Tomorrow

In a world of giggles, I wander about,
Pondering if there's a remote for doubt.
My cereal sings, each crunch a delight,
Dreaming of futures, but still stuck in tonight.

The mailman's a wizard, or so I believe,
Delivering wishes, he can't help but weave.
With a sprinkle of humor and a dash of chance,
I'll skip through tomorrow, in this silly dance.

A Journey Within

I woke up today with a giant to-do,
All my socks mismatched, what am I to do?
With coffee in hand, I face the great quest,
Finding my path, but I'm wearing a vest.

I searched for my dreams in my old shoebox,
Only found lint and a pair of red socks.
Should I chase rainbows or play hopscotch instead?
Maybe I'll join a circus, juggling bread!

The map says go left, my heart says go right,
Should I run like the wind or just hang tight?
In puddles I leap, like a daring young knight,
Wading through chaos, oh what a delight!

So here's to the journey, with humor and flair,
Who knows where I'll end up, but I don't care!
With laughter as compass, I'll conquer each lane,
For joy is the treasure in this playful game.

Embracing the Unknown

I tiptoed through life like a cat on a wall,
Wondering which way I should head for my call.
With mischief in mind and a grin on my face,
I embraced the unknown like a heckler in space.

Adventure awaits, but I lost my map,
Maybe I'll end up in the land of mishap.
With jellybeans guiding my steps as I roam,
I might build a castle out of leftover foam!

Monsters and dragons don't frighten me much,
I'll negotiate peace with a playful touch.
For in every unknown is a wise little clue,
That life is just silly, and I laugh, too!

So here's to the winding, the twists, and the turns,
Each day is a lesson; oh, how much I learn!
With giggles and chuckles, I sway through the haze,
Embracing the unknown in delightful ways.

The Art of Becoming

I tried to be wise, so I Googled the steps,
But all I found were weird cat memes and prep.
I fear life's a canvas—where's my paintbrush?
With colors a-crunched, oh, I'm in quite a rush!

Am I becoming wise, or just wildly absurd?
My thoughts like confetti—hilarious, blurred.
I'll sculpt my existence with a disco ball,
And twirl through the chaos, having a ball!

They said find your passion, I forgot my name,
But dancing in slippers, who's keeping me tame?
In socks with a purpose, I'll shuffle around,
Creating a masterpiece out of lost ground.

So raise up your glasses, let's toast to this ride,
To awkward adventures and laughter beside.
With each little slip, I'm learning to soar,
The art of becoming is never a bore!

Hints of Destiny

I found a fortune cookie left on my shelf,
It said, 'Don't take life too seriously, my elf.'
With sprinkles of fate and a cupcake in hand,
I'll follow the crumbs to the promised land!

The stars seem to giggle, they light up the sky,
Saying, 'Hey, buddy, give it a try!'
With my map of confetti and dreams all askew,
I might end up dancing in a giant shoe!

Some days I feel lost like last week's leftovers,
But I'll keep on searching in sparkly dovers.
For every mishap holds a clue in disguise,
With hints of destiny in the world's surprise.

Let's skip down the road and see what we find,
With laughter as fuel, we won't be confined.
Life is a puzzle, but I've got the zest,
Hints of my journey? Just a funny jest!

The Call of Adventure

I woke up one day, not a clue in sight,
Thinking of things that might feel just right.
Dancing with socks, on a chilly floor,
Should I make potions or maybe explore?

A cat on my shoulder, a hat on my head,
I ponder my path, and I dream of bread.
Should I be a pirate or a juggler wise?
It seems even the toast has its own surprise!

With a treasure map made of candy bars,
I'll sail through the skies, dodging all the cars.
A quest for the socks that have vanished away,
An epic adventure that starts today!

And if I get lost, I'll just ask the bees,
They always know how to find the sweet trees.
The call of excitement, and laughter that's free,
Maybe I'll find what's meant just for me.

Portraits of Tomorrow

I sit with my crayons, feeling quite grand,
Drawing my dreams with an unsteady hand.
A landscape of giggles, and candy on trees,
A splash of confetti, all bound in threes.

What will I be, an astronaut or a chef?
Maybe the king of the silly old left?
With a crown made of jelly, I'd rule with delight,
In a kingdom of doughnuts, oh what a sight!

The future's a joke, with punchlines galore,
A parade of balloons, excitement in store.
Perhaps I'll be famous for running in place,
Or hold the world record for laughter's fast pace!

With each silly sketch, my visions collide,
In the portrait of me, there's nowhere to hide.
A canvas of dreams that dances with cheer,
Tomorrow looks bright, with nothing to fear.

A Compass for the Heart

My heart's a compass, but it spins and twirls,
Pointing to cupcakes and all of the swirls.
I follow its lead, can't help but grin,
To find out where the next fun will begin!

A map full of giggles, with laughter as gold,
I chart out adventures, breaking the mold.
Should I seek the ice cream, or dance with the breeze?
The compass just giggles, "Just do as you please!"

With every wild turn, a new path to see,
I may chase the bubbles or climb up a tree.
No need for a guide, nor a point in the sky,
Just follow the rhythm, and let your heart fly!

A merry little journey that tickles my soul,
With bumps, laughs, and surprises to make me feel whole.

In the end, it's the joy that defines my decree,
And the compass leads on, oh so endlessly!

Sails of Ambition

I set my sails high, with winds that are bold,
Chasing the sunshine, let the laughter unfold.
With seagulls as mates, and snacks in the hold,
My boat is a party, in stories retold!

Should I brave the high seas or fish on the dock?
I'll keep both my options, and maybe a sock.
With pirates who giggle and treasure that gleams,
I'm sailing through life on the waves of my dreams!

An anchor of fun keeps my ship steady now,
While I juggle my plans with a whimsical cow.
Oh, the places I'll go with adventure in sight,
I'll laugh through the storms and dance in the light!

So here's to ambition, on waves made of cheer,
With every wild gust, I'll conquer my fear.
With sails full of laughter, oh what can go wrong?
This ship of mine sings the world's favorite song!

A Quest for Meaning

I wandered through a field of cheese,
Hoping to find my life's sweet tease.
But all I got were mice and ants,
Who laughed and mocked my clumsy dance.

I climbed a tree to touch the sky,
Thought I could soar but asked me why.
The branches giggled, made me yelp,
As I slid down, I found myself.

With every turn, a silly sign,
That read, 'The purpose is all mine.'
But then a squirrel threw a nut,
And I just sat there, in a rut.

I chased a cloud that looked like cake,
Tripped on my laces, took a break.
Yet in the mess, I laughed so loud,
Maybe lost, but oh so proud.

Searching for Shadows

I followed shadows deep and wide,
Thought they'd be my trusty guide.
But every time they'd slip and slide,
Beneath my feet, they chose to hide.

A black cat laughed and stole my hat,
I asked him, 'What's up with that?'
He winked and said, 'Don't take it so,
Purpose is where the sillies go!'

I danced with shadows, had a ball,
Until I tripped and took a fall.
They wrapped around, a comic sight,
Now I prance in shadows' light.

Under the sun, I made a leap,
Into a puddle, water deep.
In laughter's grasp, I learned this tale,
The journey's fun, it will prevail.

Footprints in the Fog

I wandered lost, with footless grace,
Through fog so thick, I lost my place.
Thought I'd find wisdom wrapped in mist,
But all I found was a muddy fist.

I tripped on dreams, they laughed with glee,
'Your path is hiding, wait and see!'
I questioned clouds, demanded clues,
They giggled back, and changed their hues.

A ghost appeared with shoes too tight,
'Want a dance?' he asked, quite polite.
I pirouetted, fell on my face,
Laughter echoes in this strange space.

But as I laughed, the fog slipped clear,
Revealing paths I held so dear.
In every stumble, I found a song,
Perhaps in silliness, I belong.

Seeds of Possibility

I planted seeds in my backyard,
Hoping they'd bloom, but it hit hard.
Instead of flowers, up popped weeds,
With faces squashed, they made their leads.

I gave them water, I gave them sun,
But all they did was joke and run.
'You seek your dreams? Well, good for you!
But laughter's what makes gardens grew!'

I tried to harvest wisdom ripe,
But crops of giggles shared the hype.
In every chuckle, a chance unfurled,
To find the fun in this mad world.

As seasons change, they spill their cheer,
In every blunder, love draws near.
With every giggle, my heart does sway,
I garden joy, come what may!

The Unseen Map

With crumbs and jokes, I pave my trail,
In a world that spins like a wobbly whale.
I search for signs in a barista's smile,
Sipping lattes while pondering for a while.

My GPS lost, I stroll through the park,
While squirrels giggle and leave their mark.
A dog barks loud, as if to chime,
"Hey buddy, you'll find it— just give it time!"

I tripped on my shoelace, what a nice fall,
The universe chuckled, "You'll get it, don't stall."
With a wink and a nudge, I rise up again,
Mapping my fate with each laugh and each grin.

Tomorrow may bring a spark so bright,
A path like no other, a comical sight.
So here I dance through the joy and the mess,
With a route of delight that's bound to impress.

When the Heart Murmurs

My heart whispers secrets in funny tones,
Like a saxophone solo from rattly bones.
Each giggle a clue, with each flutter a jest,
Chasing butterflies in a feather-lined vest.

It teases and tickles like old-fashioned lace,
Poking fun at me in this fickle race.
"Where's purpose, my dear?" it giggles and spins,
"Keep looking for laughter; now that's how it wins!"

At breakfast my toast sings a poppy refrain,
While the jam joins in with a sweet, silly strain.
So I'll feast on this joy, with a side of delight,
As my heart hums away into the starry night.

Tomorrow may echo this curious tune,
With more jests to savor, like a wild cartoon.
I'll waddle and wiggle, and dance on the floor,
For when laughter leads, who could want more?

Flickering Flames of Purpose

In a campfire circle, I ponder and giggle,
With marshmallows spinning, I laugh and I wiggle.
The sparks dance like dreams, playfully bright,
Whispering tales of what's possible tonight.

Each flicker tells stories of paths untold,
As I toast my ambitions like marshmallows gold.
"Charred a little? No worries!" I muse,
Life's all about finding the flavors to choose.

Then a breeze comes along like an unwelcome guest,
Sends my plans skittering; oh, what a jest!
But I lean in close, let the flames weave and swirl,
Embracing the chaos in a whimsical twirl.

Tomorrow's a canvas, with colors to splash,
In this comedy of errors, I'll make quite the clash.
With laughter as kindling, I'll stoke my own fire,
For who needs a map when you're fueled by desire?

Unfolding Horizons

With my backpack stuffed with snacks and glee,
I step outside, it's just little ol' me.
The horizon smiles like a goofy friend,
Inviting me forth, "There's fun 'round the bend!"

My compass spins wild, in absurdity's name,
Pointing to places that all look the same.
I choose left, then right, like a dance with my feet,
Finding treasure in laughter, now this is a feat!

Clouds giggle overhead, in shades of bright blue,
Whispering secrets that are funny, yet true.
So I chase down the giggles, like leaves in the air,
Embracing the chaos with curls in my hair.

Tomorrow awaits with a pile of surprises,
While I skip through adventure like joyful sunrises.
With horizons unfolding, I'm ready to roam,
For in this great puzzle, I've finally found home.

Unwritten Chapters

A blank page waits, all bright and neat,
With scribbles of dreams, oh what a feat!
I ponder life's twists, the paths I roam,
While tripping on shoes that ain't quite my own.

The coffee's cold, my plans in a spin,
Should I leap or just sit, where do I begin?
The clock keeps ticking, yet in my chair,
I write silly sonnets without a care.

My shirt's mismatched, my socks don't align,
In this circus of life, I'm the jester divine!
I'll dance with my dreams on this stage I see,
And maybe find answers disguised as a bee.

So here's to the tales that yet could unfold,
To laughter and giggles, and hot soup so bold!
For every misstep, I'll laugh and rejoice,
In this comedy show, I've found my own voice.

Flickers of Hope

A candle burns low, with wax on the shelf,
I wish it could talk, it'd talk to itself!
"Hey buddy, you flicker, what's the big plan?"
"Just trying to shine, like a good little fan."

The toast pops up; I'm grateful for bread,
As visions of grandeur float round in my head.
I'll eat till I'm full, then start something grand,
Like crafting a fortune with just one rubber band.

The cat's on the counter—my sous-chef today,
She fluffs up my hopes in her furry ballet!
So I'll sketch out a dream while the egg's going poof,
Who knew a great life could sprout from a roof?

So raise up a glass, to the winks and the blinks!
To mishaps and maybes, and lost car keys' links!
Maybe tomorrow, as the sun starts to poke,
I'll laugh at my chaos and call it a joke.

The Quest for the Why

A map in my hand, but the 'X' seems to hide,
I'm walking in circles with no one as guide.
My buddy the squirrel gives me the eye,
As I ponder the reason and let out a sigh.

"Why am I here?" I ask with a grin,
He points to a tree, 'cause that's where we begin.
I'll climb up high, just to have a good view,
And maybe discover I like it up blue!

With snacks in my pocket, adventures await,
A quest for my why, is it too late?
But fear not, dear friend, for life's full of smiles,
With goof ups and laughter to last us for miles.

So let's trip on the roots, and dance with a bee,
For the journey's the why, just hang on and see!
If the answers don't come, I might just go play,
With my trusty companions, we'll laugh all the way.

Tomorrow's Promise

The sun'll set soon, but what's on the slate?
A dance party's brewing, and I can't be late!
With half-eaten pizza and music that blares,
I'll shake off my worries, like lint from my chairs.

The clock chimes loud, it's a thrilling affair,
I've got mismatched socks and wild flowing hair.
But as the stars twinkle, I just wanna hum,
Life's vibrant tomorrow just waits for the fun.

I'll take out my crayons and sketch out a dream,
With sparkles and rainbows that glitter and gleam.
Tomorrow's promise, it's like candy on beat,
With laughter and whimsy, life's surely a treat!

So here's to the night, and all it can bring,
The joy and the chaos, oh let us all sing!
I'll hold out my hand, let's skip through the pink,
For tomorrow's in sight, while we dance and we wink!

Chasing Fleeting Light

I chased a beam that danced away,
It sparkled bright, then went astray.
I tripped on shadows, rolled with glee,
Maybe next time, it will stick with me.

A butterfly giggled, flew on a whim,
I tried to catch it—fell in the brim.
With donuts and dreams, I'll plot my schemes,
And hope tomorrow is sweeter than creams.

The sun peeked out and said, "Well, hi!"
I waved back, my spirit awry.
Life's just a dance, quite silly too,
I'll hustle and twirl, how about you?

So here's my map with doodles and flair,
A treasure chest full of laughter to share.
Who knows what awaits on this vibrant stage?
Let's sprinkle some joy, and turn the page!

A Journey Yet Unwritten

With coffee in hand, I scribble and sigh,
A blank page stares back, oh me, oh my!
Each line a mystery, a giggle or two,
I'll make the mundane feel like a debut.

A squirrel in a hat scurries by fast,
He's racing ahead, as if life's a blast.
I'll follow him closely, take notes as I go,
In this grand little romp, let's put on a show!

The stars in the night wink, playfully bright,
Whispering secrets that tickle with light.
I'll gather my thoughts, color them wild,
And pen a new tale, just like a child.

So let's launch a boat on this river of dreams,
With laughter as sails, and joy as our seams.
Each ripple we make will shimmer with cheer,
Here's to our journey, now and next year!

The Tapestry of Wishes

A tapestry woven with wishes and fun,
Each thread a giggle, a race to be won.
I sat with my dreams, they danced and they spun,
Can we weave in some donuts? Oh, let's not run!

Pineapple on pizza, a bold statement,
They riot with flavor; life's great pavement.
Patchwork of laughter, stitched tight with hope,
Let's build our castle, let's glitter and grope!

Each stitch is a story, slightly askew,
Where fairies drop secrets just for the crew.
So hand me a needle, let's get to the grind,
We'll make quite a mess, but no one will mind!

Swing wide the doors to this vibrant creation,
Laughter our fabric, binding elation.
Together we'll craft every quirky delight,
In the tapestry made of purehearted light!

Fables of What's to Come

In a land of peculiar and funny fables,
Where raccoons read books and dance on the tables.
They tell me of journeys, of whiskers and flies,
With every new story, my sensibility fries.

A frog in a waistcoat recited some rhymes,
About jumping to joy and avoiding the crimes.
"Don't worry so much; life's silly," he'd croak,
Take leaps of sheer laughter, don't just be a bloke!

Every day's chapter, a surprise for the wise,
You'll juggle your whims, and be light as the skies.
With colors that swirl, and giggles that hum,
Dare to imagine, oh, what's to come!

So slide on your socks, let your worries take flight,
Where worries are little and laughter is bright.
Let's write our fables, quite wild and fun,
With whimsy as the ink, let's start to run!

The Path Unfolds

I woke up today with socks that don't match,
A coffee spill on my favorite shirt,
Should I buy a map or embrace the chaos?
Maybe fortune favors the absurd flirt.

I tripped over my cat and fell on my face,
She looked at me like, 'What a disgrace!'
But laughter is bright, like sunshine's embrace,
My path is a dance, not a rigid race.

Is that a sign or just a weird dream?
A squirrel in a tie giving fashion advice?
I'll follow the breadcrumbs, whatever that means,
As long as there's pizza, I'll roll the dice!

Adventure awaits in a cereal box,
Where dreams leap out dressed as silly foxes.
With giggles and wiggles, I'll learn to relax,
And find joy in the unexpected detox.

Finding My North Star

I sat on a hill and looked for my muse,
A compass that points through laughter and sighs.
But all I found were ducks in a snooze,
Waddling dreams wearing winked little eyes.

Perhaps my direction is just in the breeze,
With laughter that sails on a boat made of cheese.
Forget about charts; let's loosen our knees,
And dance with the whimsy that simply won't freeze.

A potato's my mask for this hilarious quest,
If tubers have talent, we'll put them to test.
With every odd choice, I'll feel truly blessed,
In wacky pursuits, I find my zest!

So here's to the moments that make us feel light,
To finding excitement in the wildest flight.
Follow the laughter, the silliness bright,
And maybe, just maybe, I'll find my own light.

Dance of Possibilities

In the land of confusion, I wear clown shoes,
Juggling my thoughts like ripe mangoes in May.
Each slip on the dance floor, a chance to amuse,
With twirls of delight that lead me astray.

A checkered past in mismatched prints,
Where plans are a puzzle, missing some hints.
But who needs a script when you can invent?
The silliness grows like a quirky event.

I spun with a penguin, we tapped on the ice,
Each dance step a quirk, oh, isn't it nice?
They said it's absurd, should I take their advice?
But my heart's in a jig, like a kid with a slice.

So let's dance with the daisies and waltz with the bees,
Savoring joy, like fresh sunlight through leaves.
With every odd turn, I'll dive to my knees,
Embracing the chaos, wherever it leads!

Beyond the Horizon

Far past the fence where the grass is so green,
Lives a quirky old man with a pet tambourine.
He hums to the clouds, each note a routine,
As I search for a path that feels less like a machine.

With binoculars perched on his crinkly nose,
He told me of places where silliness grows.
"A taco on wheels?" As the laughter just flows,
I realized this journey's where magic bestows.

So onward I trudge with my jellybean hat,
A sprinkle of glitter and laughter to pat.
The signs say, 'Why Not?' so I'll give that a spat,
Chasing whims in the wind, here and there, like a cat.

Beyond the horizons where nonsense is grand,
Each giggle a star, I'll take a firm stand.
In a world spun with joy, like a well-mixed band,
Life's sweetest adventures, just waiting, unplanned!

The Golden Hour

In the morning sun, I chase my snack,
A muffin runs fast, I'm on its track.
Coffee in hand, I plot my day,
But the muffin's a ninja, it's gone, hooray!

With crumbs on my shirt, I sit and ponder,
To nap or to snack, oh I do wonder.
The world is a stage, a stage full of cheese,
Where I'm just a player, hoping for freebies!

The clock ticks away, but that's all right,
I'll dance through the day, from morning to night.
Each moment is gold, or perhaps just a joke,
Like me tripping over while chasing a yolk!

So here's to the hour, that glimmers and shines,
With laughter and fun, let's see what it finds.
For life's just a treasure, with treasures to buy,
As long as there's cake, I will reach for the sky!

Sailing Toward Tomorrow

I set sail today on a boat made of toast,
With a jellyfish captain who loves to boast.
The winds blow me sideways, the waves laugh and tease,
While I search for land made of pancakes and cheese.

My compass is broken, it's lost all its flair,
It points to the kitchen, full of sweet fare.
Yet the seagulls are chirping, they sing out my tune,
As I drift toward a marshmallow-filled afternoon.

With laughter and joy, I splash through the sea,
Each wave brings adventures, oh, what will they be?
The treasure map's soggy, but still holds a spot,
Where X marks the cookie, oh yes, that is hot!

So I sail with a grin, a cap made of pie,
Tomorrow can wait; let's eat cake in the sky.
For bread on the water is the best kind of fate,
As long as I'm sailing, why worry or wait?

A Voyage of Self

I packed up my dreams in a bag made of socks,
Setting sail for the land of quirky clocks.
The ship made of rubber, we floated along,
As I hummed to the tune of a pop-up song.

Self-discovery's more fun with a hat,
Especially one shaped like a flustered cat.
With each wave I ride, I ponder and muse,
Should I be a chef, or a dancing moose?

The ocean of options, it swirls all around,
But which path to take? I'm lost and I'm found.
Each island I spot has a Sign: "Try Your Luck!"
So I flip a coin, and it lands in a truck!

Life's a funny voyage, a weird, silly spree,
With hiccups and giggles, oh, just wait and see!
So off I will sail, with patches and patch,
For the journey is laughter, and plans, well, who's that?

The Secret Map

I found a map drawn in crayon and spilled juice,
X marks a treasure, but first, what's the use?
With a chocolate chip compass that points to the ruck,
I'm off on a quest, but my shoe's in a muck!

From the land of the giggles to Pudding Peak,
I'll climb with my buddies, the jellies, unique.
But wait—what's this? There's a dragon, oh snap!
He guards all the candy, my heart goes kaplap!

We dance and we twirl, to distract him with flair,
The dragon's impressed—does he even care?
With laughter and sweets, the map's just a game,
In a world filled with fun, it's all the same!

So here's to the secrets, the laughs, and the cheer,
As we search for the treats hiding somewhere near.
No need for a legend, just smiles and a knack,
For the real treasure's friendship, and that's a fact!

The Heart's Compass

Lost in a maze of socks,
Wondering which pair rocks.
The map's upside down, oh dear,
Directions smell like leftover beer.

I chase my dreams like a cat,
Dancing in circles, imagine that!
Tomorrow's plans cling like gum,
But today's laughter makes me numb.

Woke with pants of polka dots,
Search for purpose in these thoughts.
While the coffee pot gurgles cheer,
I'll flip a coin and dance with cheer.

So here's to wandering in style,
With mismatched shoes, let's compile.
Adventures await in a wild charade,
I might find sense, or just my next braid.

Echoes of Yearning

In the fridge, leftovers hum,
Pizza dreams, and then some!
Searching for answers in takeout boxes,
Maybe I'll solve it with chocolate foxes.

I ponder life over a slice,
Is playing games really so nice?
Tomorrow's wisdom left me cold,
So here I am, no plans to uphold.

Counting sheep that are out of sync,
Each one asks, "Have you had a drink?"
The past was bright, today's a mess,
Where's my guide in this odd finesse?

With socks on my hands, I take a stand,
Creativity's fault was quite unplanned.
Yet laughter echoes, bright and loud,
In chaos, I wear my quirkiest shroud.

Voices Beneath Stars

Under the stars, I trip on a shoe,
Trying to find what I should pursue.
Whispers giggle as I fumble around,
The voice of a squirrel is my favorite sound.

I asked a rock for some advice,
It just sat there, frozen like ice.
Yet the moon winked in delight,
"Keep moving, fool, till it feels right!"

Pine trees sing me a lullaby puff,
Giggles emerge when it's all too tough.
Beneath the sky, my dreams take flight,
Maybe they'll land by morning light.

My purpose is bouncing like a ball,
One day I'll catch it, that's my call.
For now, I shall dance in the deep blue,
And laugh at shadows that are so askew.

A Tapestry of Tomorrow

Weaving dreams from spaghetti strands,
Hoping to catch life's promiscuous hands.
The fork of destiny twirls my fate,
Each day arrives, just slightly late.

Juggling plans with a smile so bright,
If I drop them, I'll laugh in flight.
Life's a canvas, a messy affair,
Splashing colors really shows I care.

Accidental moves down a wild route,
Chasing purpose like a playful scout.
Tomorrow's gift may just be a rug,
Woven with quirky hugs and a shrug.

With fabric soft as whispered cheer,
I'll stitch up joy, year after year.
For every thread is wrapped in fun,
In this tapestry, I'll never be done.

Whispers of Tomorrow

I woke up this morning, not sure what to do,
Should I dance with my cat or just play with my shoe?
The fridge seems inviting, perhaps a snack spree,
But first, I need coffee, or maybe just tea!

With socks on my hands, I look quite absurd,
Trying new things, like a bird who can't bird.
The world is my stage, today I'll recite,
A monologue about how my hamsters took flight!

I spilled all my dreams in a bowl on the floor,
They scattered like marbles, but wait, there's more!
I'll catch them all later, and keep them in line,
But for now, it's a party with my pet porcupine!

So here's to tomorrow, with laughter and cheer,
Where mischief and mayhem are waiting right here.
I may just embrace what this life has to send,
For every odd moment, we'll surely transcend!

Echoes in the Dawn

The sun peeks in softly, invading my dreams,
I trip on my slippers with laughter and screams.
Such theatrics in waking, oh what a delight,
Maybe I'll juggle some pancakes today — why not try?

My coffee is brewing with moans and it sighs,
Each sip is a step towards my big surprise.
I'm sure there's a purpose in this heavy cream,
I'll find it while daydreaming, it's part of the scheme!

The cat judges my choices from atop of the chair,
She flicks her tail, as if saying, "Beware!"
Through artistic chaos, I'll paint the town red,
Or at least have a laugh while eating some bread!

So let's keep our hopes light and our minds in a whirl,
Embrace every stumble, give life a good twirl.
For echoes of laughter will guide us along,
As we stumble and fumble, let's sing our own song!

Chasing Stars in Daylight

In broad daylight, I set out for the stars,
With shoelaces tied and an army of jars.
Each jar filled with dreams, both silly and grand,
I'm off on a journey, let's see where I land!

With a hat made of foil, I'll aim for the sun,
Who knew that this quest could be so much fun?
I'll borrow my neighbor's dog — he's got good taste,
Together we'll wander, let's make haste!

Perhaps we'll discover a thing or two,
Like how to fly kites and cook kangaroo stew.
Or maybe we'll simply just nap in the grass,
After all of the frolicking, a break will not pass.

So here's to the chase, with laughter and flair,
For every wild moment, we'll surely declare.
Adventure awaits, in the light of the day,
Let's chase all the wishes that come out to play!

Threads of Fate

A sneaky little spider is weaving my fate,
While I overthink lunch, is it too late to bake?
With flour on my nose and ideas all twirled,
I'm crafting my destiny, oh what a world!

I trip over my thoughts like socks on the floor,
As history whispers of the pizza I swore.
Each thread of existence, I tangle and laugh,
Could this be the day for my sandwich autograph?

With scissors and glue, I'll create a new plan,
To maim my ambitions, but not a strong man.
You see, life's a tapestry — silly and bright,
And I'm just here cutting it all with delight.

So spin me a yarn as we flutter and flail,
With laughter our compass, we'll surely prevail.
For every misstep's a thread on our spool,
Let's stitch up our dreams and make laughter the rule!

Carving Tomorrow's Truth

With a spoon and a dream, I set out today,
To carve out my path in a clumsy way.
The woodchip flies high, my aim is quite wrong,
But laughter erupts, oh, it's where I belong.

I stumble and trip, my chisel takes flight,
Shaping a vision that dances with light.
A tree that grows upside down, how absurd,
Yet somehow it sings, or at least it's inferred.

Each tick of the clock is a giggle or two,
Painting futures with colors of silly and blue.
Who knew that tomorrow could look like this,
A masterpiece born from a perfect miss?

So I keep on carving, with joy in my heart,
Tomorrow's a canvas, I'm playing my part.
With a hand covered in chips and a grin on my face,
Tomorrow's truth winks—it's a goofy embrace.

The Soul's Unfolding

In a garden of thought, I'm pruning my mind,
With scissors and snips, I'm out there to find.
The petals of laughter start blooming so bright,
Who knew that my soul liked to wear polka dots?

I water my worries with giggles and glee,
The sun is a jester, just shining on me.
As the bees buzz with joy, dancing chase on a whim,
I twirl with the daisies, feeling utterly dim!

With each little sprout, my quirks start to show,
Turning fears into puns, a delightful tableau.
It's clear as I bask in this colorful ground,
I'm a flora of fun, in chaos, I'm found.

And maybe tomorrow, I'll bloom into cheer,
With roots made of laughter, that's perfectly clear.
So here's to the growth, and marvelous spins,
In the garden of life, joy is where it begins.

A Dance with Potential

I twirl with my dreams on a slippery floor,
Each step that I take opens another door.
With two left feet, I'm a tap-dancing star,
But the shoes are two sizes too big by far!

I spin through each tumble, a sight to behold,
Potential is dancing, in sequins of gold.
My rhythm goes wild, like a chicken on skates,
Yet the music of "maybe" joyfully waits.

With capers and chuckles, I launch into space,
A pirouette leaps, ends up in a vase.
Tomorrow's a party, with balloons filled with dreams,
Maybe they'll float, or just burst at the seams!

So bring on the fun, let's shimmy and sway,
In this dance of what's next, I'll never dismay.
Because laughing and leaping is sweet to the core,
And the beat of potential always leaves me wanting more!

Whispers of the Future

In the corners of night, I hear giggles and sighs,
Whispers of tomorrows dressed up in disguise.
Sneaky little hints hide behind closed doors,
Poking fun at my plans, as they plot and they roar.

I tiptoe around, my flashlight a beam,
Following shadows of a fabulous dream.
But confusion collides with a laugh and a tease,
As the future pranks me, it's all just a breeze.

Chasing the whispers on this comedic quest,
I dance with wild hopes, allowing some rest.
Tomorrow is sneaky; I'm here for the jibes,
With a heart full of chuckles, I'm ready for vibes!

So here's to the mischief those whispers do make,
A riddle wrapped in laughter, for goodness' sake.
With a wink and a nod, I'll embrace the unknown,
For the whispers of future are silliness grown!

In the Silence of Dawn

The alarm clock screams, it's time to rise,
With wild hair and sleepy eyes.
I dance with socks, mismatched, it's true,
Maybe today I'll find something new.

Coffee spills, I wear it well,
I'm a walking, talking, caffeine spell.
The toast pops up with a goofy grin,
Breakfast of champions, let chaos begin!

The sun peeks in, a mischievous spy,
Chasing dreams like clouds in the sky.
I trip over thoughts, they bounce and tumble,
In this nutty world, who needs to be humble?

So here I am, with giggles and cheer,
A jester in life, let's shift into gear.
Tomorrow may bring tales untold,
But for now, I'll just laugh as I unfold!

Seeds of Potential

In the garden of dreams, I plant my thoughts,
With water and sunshine, I plot my plots.
A little seed whispers, 'Oh, what a ride!'
Pulling weeds of doubt, come join me outside!

The carrots are shy, hiding in dirt,
While peas play tag, but oh, they can hurt!
I toss in some laughter, a sprinkle of zest,
In this quirky landscape, I'm feeling blessed!

Digging for answers, I unearth a shoe,
Who knew it was hiding, it's lost and blue?
The garden gnomes offer sage advice,
"Stay weird and wacky, that's our best life choice!"

So I'll cultivate joy, in patches of green,
With a twirl and a laugh, I'll keep it serene.
Each seed contains magic, just waiting to sprout,
Who knew potential was just a fun shout?

The Canvas of Days

With every brushstroke, I splash some cheer,
Coloring moments that dance ever near.
A polka dot sun with a frown on its face,
I giggle and paint it in a quirky embrace.

Clouds do the tango while raindrops do flips,
Together they make the silliest trips.
Sketching a unicorn, oh what a sight,
Just to brighten my world with laughter and light!

Each day, a canvas, splatters of fun,
Embracing the chaos, my schedule's undone.
I'll blend in the mishaps, mix laughter with strife,
Creating my masterpiece, this beautiful life!

So here's to tomorrow, whatever it brings,
May it flutter like butterflies with sparkly wings.
With humor as my palette, I'll paint it all bright,
In the gallery of days, let's dance with delight!

Navigating Winds of Change

The winds of change are a playful crew,
Tickling my plans, oh what to do?
I sail a canoe through waves of surprise,
Laughing at life and all of its lies.

A compass that spins like a top in a frenzy,
Guiding me gently through seas that are trendy.
With a wink and a nod, I adjust my sails,
Casting off worries, I'll follow the trails.

The clouds drift by in whimsical shapes,
Like kittens and cupcakes, these are my escapes.
Before I know it, I'm skimming the skies,
Waving at rainbows and telling them lies.

So here's to the winds that whisper and play,
They carry my laughter like kites in ballet.
With every gust pushing me towards the fun,
Tomorrow may wait, but today's already won!

The Turning Page

I woke up this morning, with toast in my hair,
Wondering if life's a game, or just a weird fair.
Should I chase after dreams, or just eat some pie?
The clock keeps on ticking, but I'm still asking why.

My cat looks quite wise, as she gives me a stare,
Maybe she knows secrets, just hidden somewhere.
Should I wear mismatched socks, or go for a tie?
Life's a grand play, and I'm eating the fry.

The books on my shelf stare down with a grin,
Each one has a tale, where do I begin?
I'll read with a smile, and maybe seek fun,
In this circus called life, I'll laugh till I'm done.

Reflections of the Soul

At the mirror I stand, hair wild like a crow,
Wondering deep down if I'm a weirdo,
Can a sock puppet teach me what life's all about?
Or should I just dance, with no fear, no doubt?

Chasing my thoughts like a cat with a string,
In this crazy ol' world, what fresh joy will I bring?
Maybe I'll juggle and trip with delight,
Or just bake a cake that defies all my height!

With snacks as my fuel, I'll swerve right and left,
So many wild choices, what a glorious theft!
Should I wear a clown hat, or just go with the flow?
In reflections of laughter, it's fun to just glow.

The Dance with Destiny

With two left feet and a heart full of cheer,
I'm twirling in circles as the end draws near.
Should I follow the rhythm, or stomp on the beat?
In a dance with fate, my life's bittersweet.

I stumble, I laugh, and then trip on a shoe,
The path keeps on stretching, and I don't have a clue.
Is it a waltz to the moon, or a jig to the sun?
Each step's a new journey, so let's just have fun!

The DJ is spinning a tune I don't know,
But I shimmy and shake, like a wobbly pro.
With friends by my side, we'll dance through the night,
In this wacky adventure, everything feels right.

Sacred Questions

What's the meaning of life? Oh look, a butterfly!
Should I ponder the universe or just eat some pie?
I've folded my laundry, but what does it mean?
For every lost sock, is a new fun routine?

If I ask the stars, will they laugh at my plight?
Or whisper sweet nothings about fish and delight?
Shall I ponder my fate over tacos and cheese?
Or just take a nap, with a slight breeze?

With questions galore, I'll throw caution to wind,
Every answer's a riddle, where should I begin?
Life's a puzzle of chaos, a sumptuous thrill,
In sacred confusion, I'll go in for the kill!

The Horizon Awaits

Why do we chase that bright, bold line?
It giggles and winks, an eternal vine.
I pack my snacks, a dance in my feet,
The horizon laughs at my clumsy beat.

With a map drawn in crayon, I set my course,
A chicken on a bike? Of course! Of course!
The sun is a jester, the clouds are my crew,
Who knew that grand plans could start with a stew?

Waves of confusion crash on the shore,
Yet here I am, wanting to explore.
A treasure map drawn in my mom's old pen,
Hoping there's gold beneath a pile of yen.

So off I go, on a quest for the fun,
With socks that are striped and mismatched in ton.
Tomorrow's still hiding beneath some old fluff,
But for now, let's dance—we've had just enough!

A Glimpse Beyond Today

With coffee brewed thick as a bear's warm fur,
    I ponder how I'll find the right spur.
My chair's got a squeak that sings me a song,
    If only it knew where I truly belong.

A taco stands guard at my fridge's wide door,
It whispers sweet secrets from days of yore.
I trip on my dreams, they scatter like sprinkles,
Why do my plans feel like life's silly wrinkles?

Invisible paths twist like spaghetti at lunch,
Bouncing my thoughts in a whimsical crunch.
    I doodle my worries on old napkins still,
    Maybe tomorrow, I'll climb up that hill.

So here's to the giggles, the mess, and the grin,
    With laughter as compass, let the fun begin!
Tomorrow is waiting with open wide eyes,
    But for now, let's revel in wild, wacky ties!

The Labyrinth of Hope

Inside this maze, I trip like a clown,
Chasing bright dreams in my favorite gown.
With cheese as my lantern, I giggle and sway,
Who knew hope was shaped like a giant soufflé?

My pencil stumbles on secrets to find,
Each turn of the path is tricky and blind.
A rubber chicken serves as my guide,
Laughing and clucking, it won't let me hide.

I hear tiny voices from cupboards nearby,
They tell me my journey can make a pie fly.
Through boxes and shadows, I dance with respect,
Who knew that lost socks had wisdom to project?

I promise to follow, with flair and a grin,
This labyrinth whispers, "Just jump right in!"
Though tomorrow's a puzzle, let today be bright,
Between giggles and cupcakes, everything's right!

Unraveled Strings

My life is a ball of colorful yarn,
Tangled and twisted, but oh, how they charm!
Each strand a story, some silly, some grand,
Playing hide-and-seek with a wiggly hand.

I strum on a kitten, it hums me a verse,
Why does my laughter feel so well-rehearsed?
With socks on my ears and a hat made of cheese,
I spin my own tales, doing just as I please.

The knots all around me dance like they're mad,
I try to untangle them—oh, how I've had!
But life's just a giggle, a nifty old thing,
Maybe tomorrow, I'll clip that old string.

So let the strings tangle, let laughter abound,
In the circus of life, I'm a jester renowned.
With each silly twist, the fun starts to sing,
Here's to the chaos that brightens everything!

The Light Beyond Shadows

In a world where socks go missing,
I ponder life while dishwashing.
Lost in dreams of late-night snacks,
Chasing tales on winding tracks.

Each day feels like a puzzle,
With pieces stuck in a huddle.
I search for sense in cereal boxes,
Finding wisdom in quirky foxes.

Maybe I'll be a llama tamer,
Or the next big meme creator.
With every goal, my plans derail,
But laughter's where I'll always sail.

So I dance, a chicken on parade,
In the sun, I'm unafraid.
A twirl might just spark a shift,
Tomorrow's path, a brand-new gift.

The Horizon Beckons

The grass is greener on that side,
Where dreams unfold and cats can glide.
I'll bring my map, it's kind of faulty,
But where's the fun if it's not gritty?

With tinfoil hats and grand ideas,
I'll make a fortune or face my fears.
Here's to the whims of serendipity,
And snacks that spark my creativity.

A paper plane could start a trend,
Or my half-baked thoughts might just offend.
Yet, with a smile and cheerful prance,
I'll find my way in life's silly dance.

Chasing sunsets, making s'mores,
I'll knock on fate and open doors.
Laughter carried on the breeze,
Maybe tomorrow will bring me ease.

Verses of Tomorrow

With coffee spillage on my shirt,
I sipped and planned to conquer dirt.
Pancake dreams and jammed-up toast,
In this chaos, I will boast.

A cat is plotting my next move,
With sly eyes that seem to groove.
I'll teach my goldfish how to dance,
In hopes of giving fate a chance.

Each stumble feels like art, I swear,
Life's like a sitcom, full of flair.
Who knew the road could twist and turn,
It's the detours where I truly learn?

Tomorrow's like a mystery box,
With surprises, laughs, and paradox.
I take a leap with no regrets,
Who knows what fun the day begets?

Weaving New Beginnings

I woke up tangled in my sheets,
Last night's dreams, my mind still fleets.
What if I wove a blanket bright,
Out of giggles and sheer delight?

I'll try new hairstyles, crazy and wild,
Like a toddler in style, unabashed and riled.
With mismatched shoes and an oversized hat,
Let's take on adventures, imagine that!

I'll pen my stories, mix up the plots,
Chasing unicorns and maybe some bots.
Each word a puzzle, each rhyme a jest,
Building my future, I'll be the best.

A kaleidoscope of colors and cheer,
With every sunrise, I shift my gear.
So here's to new beginnings in tow,
Let's laugh it up and let life glow!

Song of Uncertainty

I woke up today, oh what a thrill,
A to-do list that won't fit my quill.
I pondered my path, a dance of delight,
But tripped on the cat in the morning light.

My coffee's too cold, my toast has burned,
In this circus of life, I've yet to learn.
Should I chase after dreams or binge-watch a show?
Maybe I'll nap; my decision's on hold.

The world spins in circles, it's quite a mess,
The GPS says, "Turn right!" I confess.
But my brain says, "Left!" and I'm lost in thought,
Perhaps I'll just sit, and let fate be caught.

With each little giggle, I plot my next scheme,
Life's puzzle unravels, or so it would seem.
Maybe tomorrow, I'll pick a new quest,
For now, I'll just laugh, it's truly the best.

Fragments of Tomorrow

I dreamt of a dragon who liked to bake,
He made pastries that shook the ground with each shake.
I looked for my future in flour and cream,
But all that I found was a chocolate stream.

A crystal ball told me to "dance with glee,"
So I jitterbugged with my toaster, you see.
I pondered my choices with socks that don't match,
As I spun in a whirl, I toppled and crashed.

I tried to be wise like a sage on a hill,
But all that emerged was a goofy shrill.
The crystal ball laughed, "Don't take life too plain!"
So I put on a hat and embraced the absurdity train.

As fragments of laughter filled up the air,
I realized my path was just everywhere.
Tomorrow may come, or it might just not,
But the journey is silly, that's all that I've got.

Roads Less Traveled

I took a wrong turn on a road full of snacks,
With donuts and chips in grand, towering stacks.
Should I wander to candy, baked goods, or fries?
Decisions are tough when dessert's on the rise.

The path split in two, but who needs a map?
I chose to go left, and fell in a trap.
A bouncy castle awaited, bright colors and cheer,
Lost in my bouncing, I forgot why I'm here.

Unexpected detours lead to silly delights,
Like juggling with clowns on bright, starry nights.
Maybe the road less traveled is sweet,
With laughter and jests dancing under my feet.

So here in the chaos, I'm finding my groove,
With every misstep, I've something to prove.
Tomorrow can wait with its frowns and its zips,
For today, I'll just savor my candy and trips.

Illuminated Pathways

If life's a candle, I'm a bit out of wax,
Stumbling through choices like I'm in a fax.
The light flickers dim, but hey, that's okay,
I'll just follow the glow of my pet's crazy play.

A neon sign points to the "All-You-Can-Eat,"
While I wrestle with noodles and the leap of my feet.
Should I take the plunge? A buffet for one?
Or just grab a cupcake and call it a run?

The stars are my guide, but they seem rather blurry,
I'm caught in a whim, oh how I hurry!
Each pathway illuminated, a comical plight,
As I dance with the shadows, embracing the night.

With giggles and glimmers lighting my fate,
I'll find my direction, should I even wait?
Tomorrow can offer its wisdom in time,
For now, I'll just bask in this whimsical rhyme.

Embracing the Unknown

I put on my shoes, ready to roam,
With a map made of spaghetti, oh what a home!
The path is uncertain, but that's just fine,
I'll dance with the squirrels, sip on some wine.

The coffee's too strong, but who cares?
I'll surf on the sidewalk and pull off my flares!
A cat gives me directions, with a flick of its tail,
Let's hop on the bus and go sailing with whales.

Each twist of the road brings laughter and glee,
With a joke from the trees, they tickle my knee.
I might find a hat, or a unicorn's horn,
In the depths of this chaos, I feel so reborn.

So here's to the laughter, the silly delight,
As I embrace the unknown, and dance through the night!
Who knows where I'll end up, wherever it may be,
Just promise, dear friend, you'll come dance with me!

Serendipity's Embrace

Stumbled on a donut shop, sprinkles on my face,
A trip meant for veggies, now feels like a race!
With laughter and sugar, I'm feeling so free,
Serendipity whispers, 'Come party with me!'

The fortune cookie read that I'd find a new friend,
But it's just a raccoon, in my garden again.
He steals all my chips, and we laugh in the sun,
Who knew this weird critter could offer such fun?

We twirl with the daisies, so carefree and spry,
Chasing the bubbles that float through the sky.
Maybe tomorrow, we'll catch a ride on a kite,
And travel through dreams, till we run out of light.

So here's to the moments that make us feel great,
With donuts and raccoons, let's celebrate fate!
In this topsy-turvy world, oh what a craze,
Let's hop on this journey and live in a daze!

In the Silence of Choices

The clock ticks loudly as I ponder and stare,
Should I pick the red socks or the polka-dot pair?
In the silence of choices, my brain starts to fry,
A cat jumps on my lap, as if asking me why.

The toast is now burning, the dog wants to play,
I trip on my shoelace, and shout 'hip hooray!'
With butter on my shirt and a grin on my face,
I laugh at my chaos, it's my own kind of grace.

The mirror reflects me, hair wild and askew,
With a wink and a smile, I think, 'What's new?'
Tomorrow's a mystery, but today I'll just be,
A silly mess of laughter, wild and carefree!

So should I dive in or just sit on the edge?
With choices aplenty, I'll dance on this ledge.
With giggles and wobbles, I'll take each delight,
In the silence of choices, I'll shine ever bright!

Navigating the Endless Skies

With a paper airplane and a map made of cheese,
I soar through the clouds, feeling so at ease!
The GPS is broken, it sings a mad song,
But I laugh with the stars, where I truly belong.

The clouds are my playground, I tumble and flip,
Avoiding the seagulls with their mischievous quip.
I'd exchange a few giggles for dodging the rain,
For in this wild journey, I've got nothing to gain.

I spot a tall sandwich drifting by on a breeze,
It waves me to join in a luau with peas!
With lemonade rivers and cookies on trees,
Navigating the skies, my heart feels a tease.

So here I will sail, with a grin ear to ear,
Each adventure a tale, as the world disappears.
Tomorrow might beckon, with questions so sly,
But today's full of laughter, as I dance in the sky!

www.ingramcontent.com/pod-product-compliance
Lightning Source LLC
Chambersburg PA
CBHW071832160426
43209CB00003B/278